NISTIR 7516

Forensic Filtering of Cell Phone Protocols

Aurélien Delaitre
Wayne Jansen

COMPUTER SECURITY

Computer Security Division
Information Technology Laboratory
National Institute of Standards and Technology
Gaithersburg, MD 20899-8930

August 2008

U.S. Department of Commerce

Carlos M. Gutierrez, Secretary

National Institute of Standards and Technology

James M. Turner, Deputy Director

Reports on Computer Systems Technology

The Information Technology Laboratory (ITL) at the National Institute of Standards and Technology (NIST) promotes the U.S. economy and public welfare by providing technical leadership for the Nation's measurement and standards infrastructure. ITL develops tests, test methods, reference data, proof of concept implementations, and technical analysis to advance the development and productive use of information technology. ITL's responsibilities include the development of technical, physical, administrative, and management standards and guidelines for the cost-effective security and privacy of sensitive unclassified information in Federal computer systems. This Interagency Report discusses ITL's research, guidance, and outreach efforts in computer security, and its collaborative activities with industry, government, and academic organizations.

> Certain commercial entities, equipment, or materials may be identified in this document in order to describe an experimental procedure or concept adequately. Such identification is not intended to imply recommendation or endorsement by the National Institute of Standards and Technology, nor is it intended to imply that the entities, materials, or equipment are necessarily the best available for the purpose.

Abstract

Phone managers are non-forensic software tools designed to carry out a range of tasks for the user, such as reading and updating the contents of a phone, using one or more of the communications protocols supported by the phone. Phone managers are sometimes used by forensic investigators to recover data from a cell phone when no suitable forensic tool is available. While precautions can be taken to preserve the integrity of data on a cell phone, inherent risks exist. Applying a forensic filter to phone manager protocol exchanges with a device is proposed as a means to reduce risk.

Keywords: Cell Phone, Computer Forensics, Protocol Filter

Table of Contents

1. Introduction 1
2. Background 3
3. Filtering Considerations 4
4. Phone Manager Protocol Considerations 6
   4.1 Nokia PC Suite 6
   4.2 Motorola Phone Tools 7
5. Nokia Phone Manager Filtering 9
   5.1 Filter Design and Operation 10
   5.2 Filter Injection 11
   5.3 Filter Operation 13
6. Motorola Phone Manager Filtering 16
   6.1 Filter Design and Operation 17
   6.2 Filter Injection 18
   6.3 Filter Operation 19
7. Conclusions 22
8. References 23

Appendix A – Example PCS Filter Log 24
Appendix B – Example MPT Filter Log 32

Table of Figures

Figure 1: Forensic Tool Timeline 1
Figure 2: API Interception 5
Figure 3: Phone Manager Protocol Stack 6
Figure 4: FBUS Frame 7
Figure 5: Nokia PC Suite Design 10
Figure 6: Basic Operational Sequence 10
Figure 7: Filter Loaded into Nokia PC Suite 11
Figure 8: Creation of a Service with System Privileges 12
Figure 9: Starting the Service with System Privileges 12
Figure 10: Loading the Filter into Nokia PC Suite 13
Figure 11: Sequence of Operation for NPS Filtering 14
Figure 12: Motorola Phone Tools Design 17
Figure 13: Filter Loaded into mPhoneTools.exe 18
Figure 14: Injection of the Filter 19
Figure 15: Sequence of Operation for mPhoneTools.exe Filtering 20
Figure 16: Sequence of Operation for MMCenter.exe Filtering 21

1. Introduction

Over 2.5 billion cell phones are estimated in use in the world today and the number continues to grow. Digital evidence recovered from a cell phone can provide a wealth of information about the user, and technical advances in device capabilities generally offer opportunity for recovery of a broader range of information. Numerous forensic tools abound for automatic data recovery from cell phones. While the outlook should be positive, a number of factors have coalesced to impede progress in cell phone forensics. A key issue is the delay between the availability of a cell phone to the public and support for the phone by a forensic tool.

When a new phone appears, a forensic tool manufacturer must decide whether to adapt its tool for the phone, purchase exemplars for study, create and test an update containing support for the phone, and finally release the tool update to the user. The decision factors involved include the popularity of the phone model, the requirements of the customer base, and the overall support objectives of the company. The time required for needed tool updates to reach users, therefore, can be lengthy and for the least popular models may never occur. Validation of the updated tool for use in casework increases the delay, putting forensic specialists further behind the power curve of having a suitable means for automated data recovery. Figure 1 illustrates the situation.

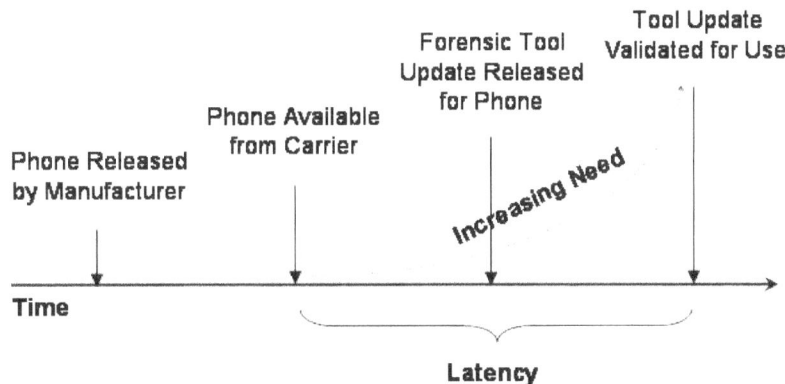

Figure 1: Forensic Tool Timeline

Phone managers are sometimes turned to as a way to recover data when no suitable forensic tool is available. Phone managers are typically available from the manufacturer of the cell phone and kept up to date with support for newly released models. They allow various operations, including retrieval of core user data such as phonebook entries and photos. The forensic soundness of tools not designed specifically for forensic purposes are questionable, however [4]. In particular, phone managers have the ability to both read and write data to a phone, which is problematic from a forensic perspective, if used without applying proper testing and procedural controls. Many anecdotes exist of a practitioner accidentally or unknowingly writing data to a phone when using such a tool.

To simplify the content recovery process, a forensically-sound access method would exist across all cell phones. More realistically, cell phones would support a common interface and protocol standard for handset communications that could be used for data recovery. A recently proposed standard from the Open Mobile Terminal Platform (OMTP) specifies the use of micro USB (Universal Serial Bus) as a universal, cross-manufacturer cable interface for power and communications. Its data synchronization capabilities might eventually provide an opportunity for a more consistent means of content recovery, if adopted by manufacturers.

Until then, avenues to reduce latency need to be pursued. For example, tool manufacturers could improve their relationships with phone manufacturers or network carriers to gain a head start on development before phones are available to the general public. Another approach to reduce latency, called phone manager protocol filtering, is described in this paper. The idea is to build on the functionality of available phone managers by augmenting them with a protocol filter that limits their functionality to allow only safe exchanges to occur.

2. Background

More than a billion cell phones were sold worldwide in 2007 and projections beyond continue to rise. Over the last decade the capabilities and features of cell phones, such as increases in performance and storage capacity, and additions of document and multimedia handling functionality, have also continued to improve rapidly, turning cell phones into data reservoirs with the capability to hold a broad range of personal and organizational information.

Forensic software tools are the preferred means for recovering digital evidence from supported cell phones. Data recovery is usually carried out through logical instead of physical acquisition, using one or more protocols supported by the device. The protocols include standardized and proprietary device synchronization protocols, command interface protocols, and diagnostic protocols.

The number and variety of phone models unveiled on the world market each year is considerable, creating a burden for forensic tool manufacturers to keep their product coverage up to date. Models introduced into one national market can be used elsewhere by replacing the identity module of a phone (e.g., a Groupe Spécial Mobile (GSM) subscriber identity module) with one from another carrier, or through roaming features. Models of older functioning phones, though out of date, can also remain in use for years after their initial release.

Unlike the situation with personal computers, mobile phone manufacturers often employ different proprietary operating systems and storage structures. New phone models often have functional differences from previous models that must be taken into account to recover and report data properly. Complicating matters further are variations in data storage location assignments, which can occur in a specific model of phone subsidized and supplied by different network carriers, due to adaptations made for the carriers by the manufacturer. Firmware updates sent out by a network carrier can also affect data locations, creating additional hurdles for developing and maintaining a tool [3].

Six manufacturers control about 80% of the cell phone market at any one time, while approximately forty others compete for the remaining 20% share. Nokia and Motorola led the group in 2006 with more than 50%; in 2007 Nokia and Samsung were in front with more than 50% [1, 2, 10]. New manufacturers occasionally enter the marketplace and others leave. For example, the iPhone from Apple was a new entrant in 2007.

Cell phone manufacturers such as Nokia, Motorola, and Samsung normally keep their phone manager software up to date for new and current phone models in the product line. Forensic specialists have long recognized the potential for phone managers as a tool for automated recovery of common types of core user data. Because phone managers are not forensically sound, additional steps must be followed to use them to recover data. They include validating the operation of the phone manager, testing and verifying the procedures to be followed for acquisition to safeguard against altering data on the phone, and producing a cryptographic hash of acquired data objects.

Regrettably, even an experienced forensic specialist taking all available precautions could accidentally write data to a phone using a phone manager. Phone manager protocol filtering helps to safeguard against accidental modifications to data on the phone and provides a stopgap measure until a forensic tool update that supports the phone in question becomes available.]

3. Filtering Considerations

Forensic cell phone tools often recover data employing the same protocols used by phone managers. To avoid the problem of altering data on a phone, forensic tools restrict the protocol used to communicate with the device to only functions that are either known to be safe or involve very minor forensic issues. A potential way to gain the same advantage for phone managers is to apply a filter between the phone manager application and the device being managed that blocks harmful protocol commands from propagating. Filtering is an often used technique in computer forensics, commonly implemented in hardware or software write blockers for disk and USB device interfaces.

Most phone managers run under the Windows operating system and are distributed in binary form for installation. Communications with cell phones occur over a serial COM or USB port. Most serial port data transmission for Windows systems is done the same way as writing to a file. For example, the WriteFile function can be used to send data via a serial COM port. The same function also works with virtual serial ports established over USB, infrared, or Bluetooth communications. The technique used for the filter prototype involves intercepting the call from the phone manager to the Application Programming Interface (API) for this function to capture the data, interpret the content, and return an appropriate response to the phone manager. Similarly, calls to other related functions, such as CreateFile and ReadFile, would need to be intercepted for the filter to work overall.

API hooking is a term used to describe intercepting calls to a function for some purpose, usually to customize and extend its functionality and also to monitor aspects of an application. The target function may be in an executable application, a library, or a system Dynamic Link Library (DLL). In the case of Windows operating systems, the functions of interest are part of the so-called Win32 API. Hooking Win32 APIs is not new; security add-ons, such as personal firewalls and anti-virus applications, as well as malicious code, such as rootkits, have used these techniques to insert themselves seamlessly into an operating system. The interception process is performed at run time against a running process rather than modifying static binary images at rest.

Several different techniques have been used to hook Windows APIs. A common way is to alter the Import Address Table (IAT) of a given module and replace the target function with the substitute function. The IAT contains the address of each imported function and is used by the loader to map function calls to entry points of loaded routines. Alternatively, an unconditional jump can be inserted in the first few bytes of a target function to change the flow of execution to the substitute function. When the substitute function completes its task, control is returned to the modified function or, optionally, back to the calling program.

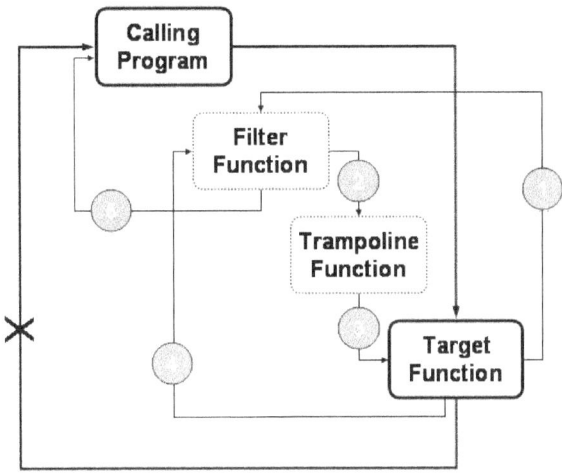

Figure 2: API Interception

The approach used for the phone manager filter is to have the substitute function serve as a wrapper for the target function, as illustrated in Figure 2. The first few instructions of the target function are replaced with a jump to the filter function, and the replaced instructions from the target function are preserved in a so-called trampoline function [6]. The trampoline function acts like a relay, ending with a jump back to the target function to complete processing after the preserved instructions are executed. The filter function can either call the trampoline function to invoke the target function, or return directly to the calling program and bypass the target function altogether. The target function is also adjusted to return control to the filter function upon completion to allow the filter to perform any needed post function operations.

The use of this technique makes the filter somewhat system-dependant. Certain functions of the Win32 API are partially overwritten. The binary code of the Win32 API can also vary with the version of the operating system. The operation also must observe the right alignment with the next, not overwritten instruction. It is typically a simple task to adapt the filter to a particular release of Windows, including the version of its service pack.

4. Phone Manager Protocol Considerations

The protocols used by a phone manager to manipulate the content of a cell phone can differ between manufacturers. Both wired and wireless means of communications may be supported. A number of protocols have been standardized for this purpose, including the AT Command set, Synchronization Markup Language (SyncML), Object Exchange Protocol (OBEX), and Infrared Data Association (IrDA) standards. In practice, a mix of standardized and proprietary protocols may be involved. The protocols used by two different phone managers to communicate with supported handsets over a serial cable are discussed in the remainder of this section. The examples illustrate some of the factors involved when filtering such protocols.

4.1 Nokia PC Suite

The Nokia PC Suite (PCS) provides a good example of a candidate phone manager for protocol filtering. The current version for the U.S. market supports approximately 75 models, including the very latest. The versions for other countries support about the same number of models, some of which are different from the models in the U.S. version. PC Suite can be used for a number of things, including copying personal data (e.g., phonebook entries) to a computer for safekeeping; transferring images, video clips, and other files from the phone to a computer; and viewing contacts and messages on a device. Certain features work only when used with those models of Nokia phones that employ compatible functionality. Various types of communications with the phone are supported, including serial COM and USB cables. Wireless options also exist.

The Nokia PCS uses a proprietary protocol called the FBUS protocol to perform its functions. An AT modem command is sent to the phone to switch into FBUS mode. The FBUS protocol is used to extract the model number of the phone, presumably to determine how to proceed. The FBUS protocol can also be used to recover other information, such as the phonebook, call logs, SMS messages, and calendar entries. Another protocol, OBEX, which rides over the FBUS frames, is also used to extract media files, ring tones, and downloaded applications that are present. The physical interface is a bidirectional serial communication bus that runs at 115,200 bps [7]. Figure 3 illustrates the situation.

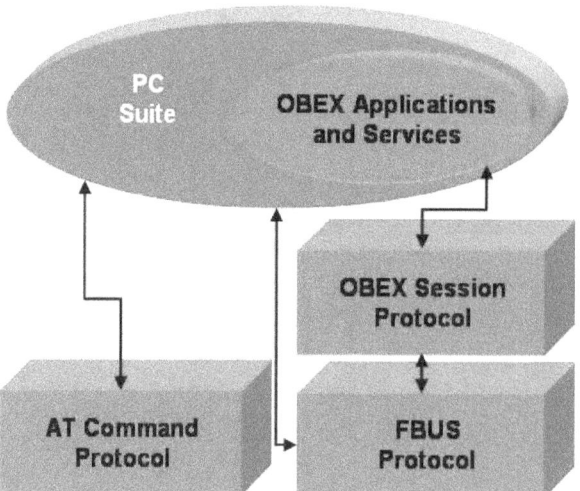

Figure 3: Phone Manager Protocol Stack

The FBUS frame is byte oriented. The first byte of the frame, byte 0, holds the hexadecimal value of the identifier for the FBUS protocol. The value 1E is the frame identifier for cable. Bytes 1 and 2 respectively contain the destination and source addresses [7, 8]. For data sent to the phone, the destination address is 00. The source address for the personal computer is 10 or 0C. Byte 3 contains the command identifier, which potentially supports up to 256 (i.e., 2^8) commands. Bytes 4 and 5 hold the length of the data that follows. The bytes following byte 5 convey the data segment of the frame. The last byte of the data segment contains a 3-bit sequence number and fragment flag, while the penultimate byte indicates the remaining frames to go to complete the payload. The last two bytes of the frame contain a checksum [7, 8]. Only frames of an even length are transmitted. A byte of all zeros is inserted before the checksum, if needed, to make the total length of the frame even. Figure 4 illustrates the frame composition.

Byte	0	1	2	3	4 - 5	6 - n	n+1 - n+2
Contents	Frame ID	Destination	Source	Command	Length	Data	Checksum

Figure 4: FBUS Frame

The FBUS protocol is an acknowledged request-response protocol, with the phone manager issuing command requests and the phone answering [7, 8]. Responses use the same command identifier as the request being answered, but reverse the source and destination address. Every request or response, except for the first request, is prepended with an acknowledgment frame indicating receipt of the last protocol element sent by the other party. This convention means that for a blocked request, the filter may need to forge a receipt acknowledgment, in addition to an appropriate negative response, to prevent the phone manager from resending a disallowed frame.

Because the FBUS protocol is proprietary, the function of all command identifiers is not known. However, over the years many of the commands have been determined through experimentation by various parties. Furthermore, the communications of forensic tools, such as the ones mentioned above, can be monitored to identify commands considered safe by tool manufacturers. To avoid propagating frames containing unsafe commands to a phone, the phone manager filter incorporates a white list of known commands considered safe; all other command frames are blocked.

OBEX performs a function similar to HTTP for devices that are resource constrained. OBEX consists of the following pieces:

- An object model that conveys information about the objects being sent, as well as the objects themselves
- A session protocol, which uses a binary packet-based client/server request-response model

The OBEX File Transfer Protocol (OBEXFTP) service is used to access the file structure of the device. The OBEX Object Push (OBEXOBJECTPUSH) service is used to exchange objects such as VCard and VCalendar and, for some devices, to access to the file structure. In addition, other proprietary methods can be defined by the manufacturer.

4.2 Motorola Phone Tools

Motorola is another major actor in the cellular phone industry. The company provides a software solution, called Motorola Phone Tools (MPT), which supports about 300 phone models. MPT offers another example of a candidate phone manager for protocol filtering.

Depending on the phone and its capabilities, MPT allows the management and synchronization of phonebook and calendar data as well as transferring copies of image, audio, video, and other files to and from the phone. MPT also provides some connectivity features, like sending SMS and MMS messages and also using the phone as a modem to connect to the Internet.

MPT can connect to a phone via cable, Bluetooth, or infrared. Motorola phones and software communicate initially by means of the AT protocol. For some operations, such as copying media files, the OBEX protocol is used instead. A specific AT command is used to switch to OBEX. The OBEX session is then established. When the session is ended through an OBEX disconnect command, the phone and software switch back to AT.

The AT command set is based on the original Hayes modem commands. The original command set has been expanded and standardized for use with cell phones to allow core data to be stored or retrieved as well as other actions (e.g., [13]). The extended commands are strings of text that generally follow the format "AT" (i.e., the attention code), followed by a command mnemonic prefixed with a plus sign, ending with any required parameters prefixed with an equal sign and separated by commas (e.g., AT+cmd=para1, para2). A response is expected for each request issued. Commands can be issued together as a string of commands using a semicolon as a separator. The standard also allows for the definition of manufacturer-specific extensions.

5. Nokia Phone Manager Filtering

As of release 6.84.10.3, Nokia PCS is made of several standalone programs. The Graphical User Interface (GUI), LaunchApplication.exe, allows the user to start the other operational sub-programs such as PCSync2.exe and ContactsEditor.exe, used respectively to synchronize data with a computer and to edit phonebook entries. These programs establish communication over a Remote Procedure Call (RPC) channel with the resident service of PCS, called ServiceLayer.exe. This service is started automatically by the operating system and is responsible for communicating with the phone. It makes use of the different protocols supported by Nokia phones (i.e., AT, FBUS, and OBEX over FBUS).

PCS can be envisaged as two distinct parts: the application, which bundles the GUI and the operational sub-programs, and the service layer, which is a sub-layer of the application. Figure 5 illustrates the design. The upper-level applications run with the privileges of the user executing them. In contrast, the service layer runs with System privileges, which gives it total access to the operating system and the resources of the computer. It is also well protected against interference from a regular user's program, since the operating system prevents a process with regular privileges from accessing the address space of another process, unless they belong to the same user. That is, a regular process cannot read or write the memory allocated by or for a process having System privileges. Other restrictions also exist, including the interdiction for a lower-privilege process to create a thread or allocate memory in an upper-privilege process.

The PCS service uses the Win32 API provided by the operating system. In this case, to communicate with a Nokia 6101 device, it uses a variant of the CreateFile function, CreateFileA[1], to get a handle on the serial port to which the phone is connected. In the main thread, the service runs a loop that scans for available devices on a regular basis. Once a device is detected, it calls CreateFileA to open a communication channel to the device. The functions WriteFile and ReadFile are used respectively to send requests to the phone and to receive the responses. Depending on the upper-level application being used, several threads are created to send requests over the newly created channel. A different thread is used to read the responses from the device using the functions ReadFile and GetOverlappedResult. GetOverlappedResult is used to read the data after a call to ReadFile to accommodate the asynchronous communication channel to the phone.

---

[1] This function takes as parameter an ASCII string describing the path to the file or the resource to be opened – hence the "A" suffix for ASCII.

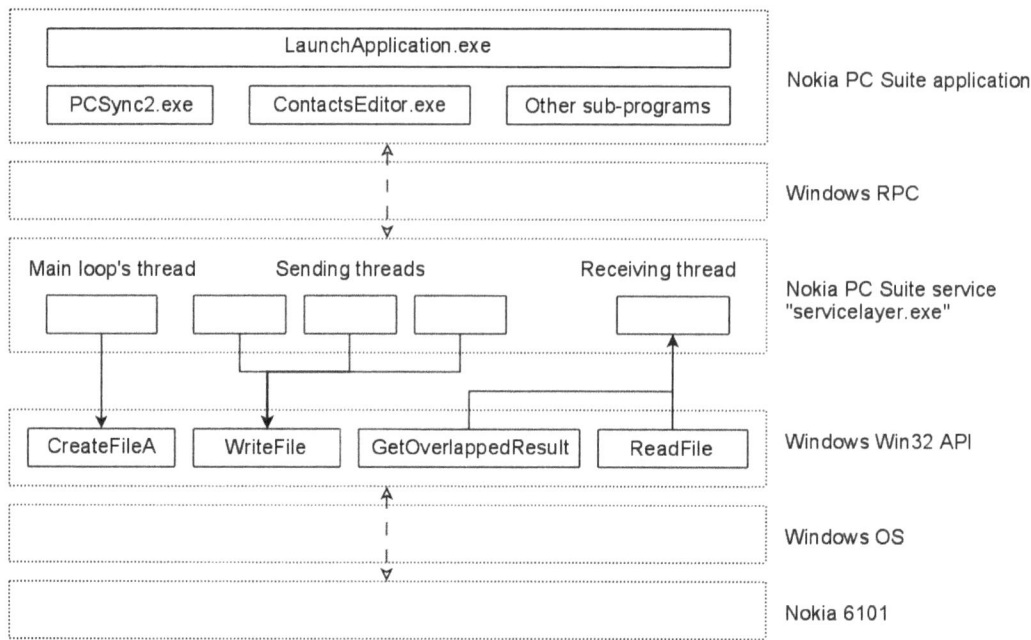

Figure 5: Nokia PC Suite Design

In the beginning of a data exchange, the phone is in the default AT mode. PCS sends the standard AT command "at&f" to initialize the phone's modem, followed by a second non-standard AT command, "at*nokiafbus", to have the phone switch to the FBUS mode. Using FBUS, PCS requests the phone's model. For example, for a Nokia 6101, the application asks for the phone capabilities using an OBEX over FBUS session. The phone replies with an XML file containing the requested information. The rest of the operations are performed, ending with an FBUS command that switches the phone back to the default AT mode, as outlined in Figure 6.

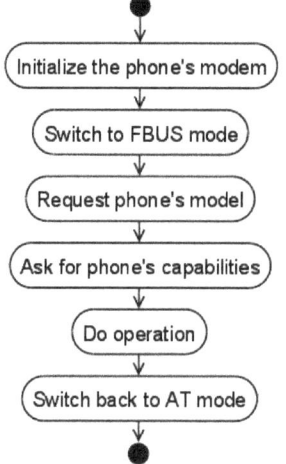

Figure 6: Basic Operational Sequence

5.1 Filter Design and Operation

The filter is injected in the memory of the service layer, ServiceLayer.exe. It serves as a wrapper for the Win32 API, intercepting the calls to the functions used to communicate with the phone, as illustrated in

Figure 7. Instead of calling the genuine function of the Win32 API, the service calls the matching detour functions of the filter. The filter then decides how to handle calls to the Win32 API.

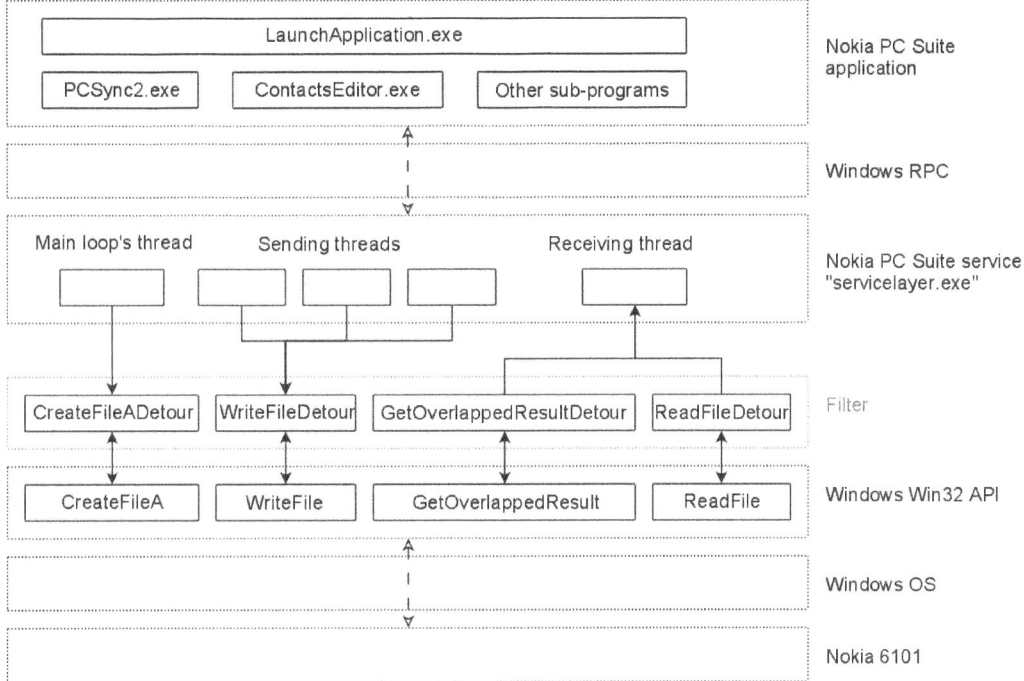

Figure 7: Filter Loaded into Nokia PC Suite

During a data exchange, PCS controls the whole operation, sending requests for the phone to answer. Hence, the filtering is done primarily by analyzing the data sent to the phone by the computer (i.e., through the intercepted WriteFile function). Unsafe requests are blocked and an error status is returned, but they also could be used to trigger a negative response (e.g., object unavailable) from the filter.

The responses sent back by the phone are not blocked by the filter. The filter does analyze and log them, using the intercepted ReadFile and GetOverlappedResult functions, before forwarding them onto the service layer. If an unsafe request is blocked, the phone will not receive it and therefore will not send back any response. Since blocked requests are not received by the phone, no responses are sent back. In general, there should be no need to filter the data sent to the computer by the phone.

5.2 Filter Injection

The filter consists of a DLL, which is loaded into the service layer's address space by a loader. The goals of the loader are to find the right process to inject, namely ServiceLayer.exe, and to load the DLL into its memory.

Since the service layer runs with System privileges, the loader also needs System privileges to carry out its work. System privileges are not granted to regular users, or even administrators, on Windows computers. Obtaining such privileges requires taking advantage of the administrators' ability to create new services [9]. A member of the Administrator group needs to create a service that runs a command prompt (i.e. "c:\windows\system32\cmd.exe") with System privileges. The Service Create tool (Sc.exe) with the syntax *sc Command Servicename [Optionname= Optionvalue...]* is used, as shown in Figure 8 [11].

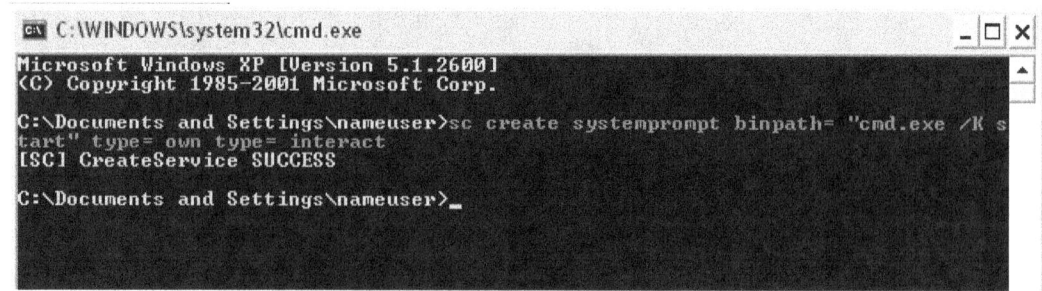

Figure 8: Creation of a Service with System Privileges

Once this new service is created, it can be started at any time to launch a System level command shell, as shown in Figure 9.

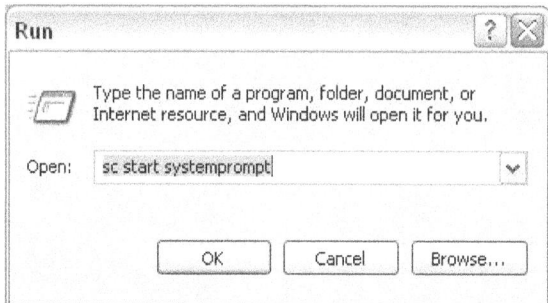

Figure 9: Starting the Service with System Privileges

From the command shell, the user navigates to the directory containing the filter's DLL and the loader, as shown in Figure 10. Before running the loader, it is necessary to ensure no phone is connected to the computer. It is safer to stop PCS's service first and then start it again, before loading the filter.

```
C:\WINDOWS\system32\cmd.exe
Microsoft Windows XP [Version 5.1.2600]
(C) Copyright 1985-2001 Microsoft Corp.

C:\WINDOWS\system32>cd /d "e:\My Documents\Visual Studio 2005\Projects\NPSfilter
\release"

E:\My Documents\Visual Studio 2005\Projects\NPSfilter\release>sc stop servicelay
er

SERVICE_NAME: servicelayer
        TYPE               : 110  WIN32_OWN_PROCESS (interactive)
        STATE              : 3  STOP_PENDING
                                (STOPPABLE,NOT_PAUSABLE,IGNORES_SHUTDOWN)
        WIN32_EXIT_CODE    : 0  (0x0)
        SERVICE_EXIT_CODE  : 0  (0x0)
        CHECKPOINT         : 0x0
        WAIT_HINT          : 0x0

E:\My Documents\Visual Studio 2005\Projects\NPSfilter\release>sc start servicela
yer

SERVICE_NAME: servicelayer
        TYPE               : 110  WIN32_OWN_PROCESS (interactive)
        STATE              : 2  START_PENDING
                                (STOPPABLE,NOT_PAUSABLE,IGNORES_SHUTDOWN)
        WIN32_EXIT_CODE    : 0  (0x0)
        SERVICE_EXIT_CODE  : 0  (0x0)
        CHECKPOINT         : 0x0
        WAIT_HINT          : 0x0
        PID                : 2212
        FLAGS              :

E:\My Documents\Visual Studio 2005\Projects\NPSfilter\release>NPSfilterLoader.ex
e
Process 'ServiceLayer.exe' has PID 2212
buffer = 00F90000

E:\My Documents\Visual Studio 2005\Projects\NPSfilter\release>
```

Figure 10: Loading the Filter into Nokia PC Suite

Once the filter is loaded, the phone can be plugged and used along with PCS. It is not possible to unload the filter once it is injected. The only safe way to resume the regular work of PCS is to stop its service and start it again, as described above.

5.3 Filter Operation

The operation of the filter is illustrated in Figure 11. The filter is first activated when the main loop of the PCS service tries to open a device, while scanning for a connected phone. PCS calls the Win32 function CreateFileA, which jumps straight to the filter's CreateFileADetour. The filter then calls the genuine Win32 CreateFileA function to open the file, as expected by the caller. If the operation is successful, the name of the open file or device is tested and, if it happens to be a serial device, the filter stores the resulting handle for later use. In the last step, the handle is returned to the caller.

Later, when an upper-level application asks for an operation to be performed on the phone, a new thread is created by the service to send a request through the previously opened device. This thread calls WriteFile to send the data and, since this function is intercepted, jumps to the filter's WriteFileDetour. If the handle to be written to is the same as the handle saved by CreateFileADetour, the caller is trying to send data to the phone. The request is analyzed by the filter to determine whether it is safe or not. If it is safe, the data is sent through the handle, by calling the genuine Win32 WriteFile, and the status of the operation is returned to the caller. If it is unsafe, then the data is not forwarded to the phone and an error status is returned to the caller, as if the execution of WriteFile failed.

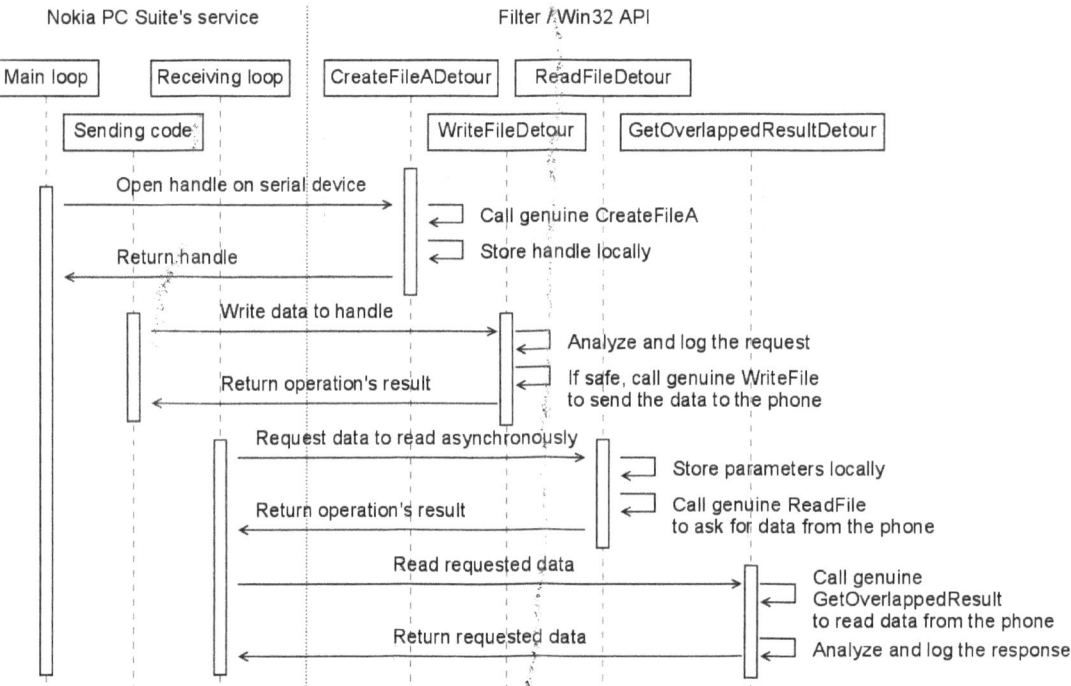

Figure 11: Sequence of Operation for NPS Filtering

The service layer has a thread dedicated to reading asynchronously received data coming from the phone. From within a loop, it asks for data to read by calling ReadFile, and then tries to actually read it with a call to GetOverlappedResult. During the first call, the filter's function ReadFileDetour is executed in place of the expected Win32 function. The filter stores the parameters of this reading request for later use by GetOverlappedResultDetour. It then calls the genuine ReadFile function and returns the status of the operation. If it is successful, the service calls GetOverlappedResult and executes the filter's GetOverlappedResultDetour function, which jumps to the genuine Win32 function. When returning, the read data is analyzed and logged by the filter, and then forwarded to the calling service.

The whole data exchange between the phone and the computer is analyzed. Every event of interest is logged in the file C:\NPSfilter.log. For example, if a frame is not understood, it is blocked and the action logged along with a dump of the frame. When a frame is allowed through, it is appended to the log file, with much of the data translated to a human-readable form. Appendix A contains an example log file with annotations.

The log file is not accessible during the operation of PCS, due to access restrictions imposed by the operating system. The filter must be unloaded for the file to be open, requiring the PCS service layer to be stopped.

Initially, the protocol analyzer is in the AT mode, as is the PCS service. When a frame is sent to the phone, the analyzer checks if the frame starts with the AT header and if it is complete and valid. Then the AT command contained in the frame is compared to the commands allowed through the filter. If there is a match, processing specific to each command is performed. The frame is reported as safe and the function WriteFileDetour sends it to the phone. Otherwise, the frame is reported as unsafe and

WriteFileDetour drops the frame by returning an error code to the calling procedure. In the case of the "at*nokiafbus" command, the specific processing includes switching the filter to the FBUS mode.

The FBUS analyzer performs basic integrity checks on FBUS frames sent by PCS. The command code is analyzed, as described in Figure 4. For each code, a list of allowed payloads is searched for matching data. If an occurrence is found, the frame is reported as safe and sent to the phone by WriteFileDetour. Otherwise, the frame is dropped. The allowed payloads are described by discriminating signatures containing wild-card characters. If the command instructing the phone to switch back to the AT mode is sent, the filter then switches back to the AT mode.

OBEX traffic can also be sent over FBUS, using specific command codes in the frame's header. In this case, the FBUS analyzer first checks the FBUS frame before feeding the data to the OBEX analyzer. Depending on the command code in the OBEX header, the frame is reported as safe or not. The only operations allowed by the filter are connect, disconnect, get, set path, and abort.

The responses sent by the phone are more complex to analyze. When in the AT mode, the frame is read character by character. Therefore, it is necessary to store the incomplete data until the whole frame has been received. After each read operation, the data goes through a fast analyzer, which determines whether or not the frame is complete. It then passes through the regular analyzer where it is logged. No filtering is performed for AT responses, which are considered harmless from a forensic point of view.

For FBUS responses, the header is read first, followed by the payload. The incomplete frame has to be stored until it is fully received. A fast analyzer determines if the frame is complete or not. Complete frames are fed to the FBUS response analyzer to be checked and logged; incomplete frames are discarded. A common problem is the recurring loss of synchronization in the FBUS traffic. Often, some frames are not yet completely read when a new one starts to be received. To resynchronize processing, whenever new FBUS traffic is available, a quick analysis is done to determine if it is the beginning of a new frame or the continuation of an incomplete one.

Another complication with FBUS is OBEX traffic riding over it. OBEX responses tend to be large, since they often contain XML or media files. It is not unusual to see an OBEX response split into many FBUS frames. Therefore, the FBUS filter stores the OBEX data it receives until a fast analyzer determines that the frame is complete. The OBEX response then passes through the OBEX analyzer to be checked and logged.

6. Motorola Phone Manager Filtering

Version 4.0 of MPT, the latest release available during this effort, was used. The software is made of three programs: mPhoneTools.exe, MOffice.exe, and MMCenter.exe. The main program, mPhoneTools.exe, is in charge of the GUI, communications, and other features. The remaining two subprograms are launched transparently from the GUI of mPhoneTools.exe, according to the actions the user wants to perform. MOffice.exe allows the user to manage the phonebook and calendar, to synchronize the computer and the phone, and to backup and restore data. MOffice.exe depends on mPhoneTools.exe for communications with the phone. The communication between MOffice.exe and mPhoneTools.exe was not studied in depth, since protocol filtering could be carried out directly in mPhoneTools.exe. The other subprogram, MMCenter.exe, is standalone and able to communicate independently with the phone to transfer files.

To perform its functions, mPhoneTools.exe, and implicitly MOffice.exe, rely on the AT protocol. Unlike mPhoneTools.exe, MMCenter.exe operates with the phone over OBEX exclusively. All of the MPT programs run with no specific privileges.

MPT uses the Win32 API and the Telephony API (TAPI32) of the Microsoft Windows operating system. The Motorola phones are recognized by Windows as modems. Their drivers follow the UNIMODEM architecture, defined by Microsoft as a standard way to describe these devices. Therefore, a program willing to communicate with the phones needs to use TAPI32.

TAPI32 allows a program to open a line, which is basically an asynchronous communication channel to a modem. MPT uses the lineGetID function – in its ASCII variant lineGetIDA – to get a handle on the line related to the phone. Then, the standard I/O functions are used to read and write data asynchronously to and from this communication channel.

mPhoneTools.exe uses the Win32 functions ReadFileEx and WriteFile for reading and writing to the channel, notably to support MOffice.exe activities. To address asynchronicity, mPhoneTools.exe checks for available data to read using the function ClearCommError. It then makes certain that reading operations have finished by calling SleepEx, which calls the completion routines for pending reads. When calling ReadFileEx, mPhoneTools.exe provides a completion routine that SleepEx uses to signal that a pending read is finished. When the completion routine is executed, it takes the necessary steps to process the data or to let the program process the data when the call to SleepEx completes.

MMCenter.exe works a bit differently. It uses the functions WriteFileEx and ReadFile to write and read data. It also uses ClearCommError to check for available data to read.

mPhoneTools.exe uses the CreateProcess function to execute the two subprograms as shown in Figure 12, along with the other Win32 APIs mentioned above.

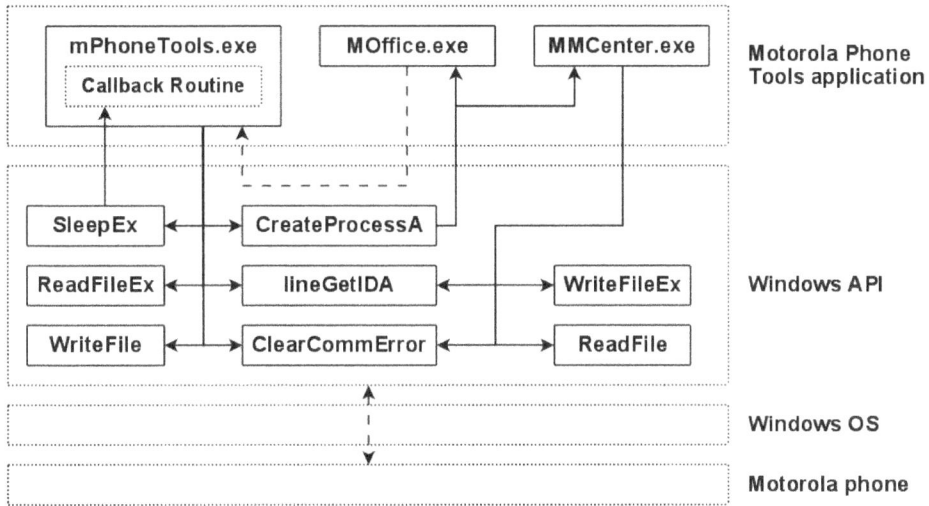

Figure 12: Motorola Phone Tools Design

The phone's modem is in AT command mode by default. Most of the operations are carried out using the AT protocol. When MMCenter.exe needs to perform operations via the OBEX protocol, it sends the AT command AT+MODE=22, which causes the phone switch to OBEX mode. The program then establishes an OBEX session and performs its task. MMCenter.exe uses the OBEX DISCONNECT frame to end the session, which also causes the phone to switch back to AT mode.

6.1 Filter Design and Operation

In contrast to the Nokia PC Suite, MPT does not use a central process to handle communications with the phone. Therefore, the filter needs to be injected in each process spawned by MPT. These processes are created using the CreateProcessA function of the Win32 API. The filter has a matching detour function, which handles its auto-injection when the subprograms MOffice.exe and MMCenter.exe are executed. Actually, MOffice.exe does not need to be injected, since all its communications go through mPhoneTools.exe, where the filter is initially loaded. Nonetheless, the filter is loaded into this program to make certain that no other process is created by MOffice.exe without being injected.

The TAPI32 function lineGetIDA is used by both mPhoneTools.exe and MMCenter.exe to open the line to the phone. To filter only this communication channel, the function is wrapped and the resulting handle is copied during its execution. Later on, this handle is compared to the handle provided to the WriteFile and WriteFileEx detour functions by the calling program. If it matches, then the data needs to be analyzed and filtered. WriteFile and WriteFileEx are used respectively by mPhoneTools.exe and MMCenter.exe to send requests to the phone. The filtering is done by analyzing the data provided to these functions and directed to the phone.

If a request is blocked, a forged response needs to be provided to the calling program to have it treat the operation as though it succeeded. To do that for MMCenter.exe, the functions ClearCommError and ReadFile need to be wrapped with the forging functionality. For mPhoneTools.exe, wrapping ClearCommError, ReadFileEx, and SleepEx in a similar way is necessary.

Figure 13 illustrates the filter serving as a wrapper for the critical Windows API functions used by MPT, when injected into the mPhoneTools.exe application.

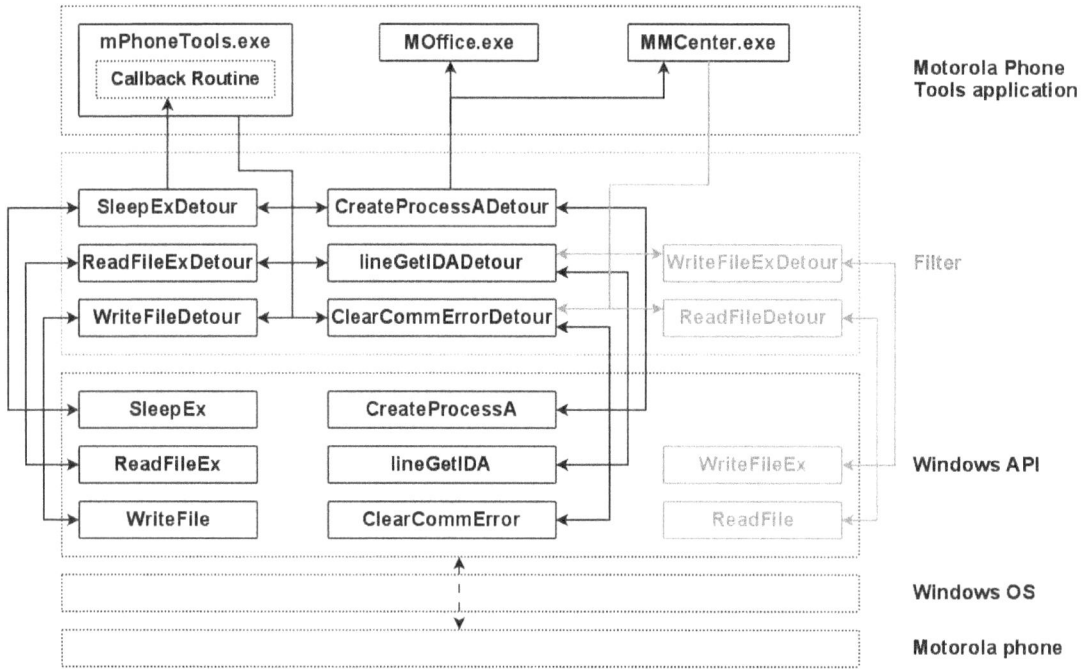

Figure 13: Filter Loaded into mPhoneTools.exe

6.2 Filter Injection

As with PCS, the filter consists of a DLL that needs to be injected. DLL injection is carried out for this filter as follows:

- A buffer in the memory of the target process is allocated using the function VirtualAllocEx.
- The name of the DLL is copied into this buffer with the function WriteProcessMemory.
- A thread is created in the target process using the CreateRemoteThread function, whose entry point is the function LoadLibraryW and whose parameter is the buffer containing the name of the DLL to inject.
- When this new thread runs in the target process, the filter's DLL is loaded by the LoadLibraryW function.

The initial injection of the filter into MPT is straightforward. First, mPhoneTools.exe has to be started. When the profile selection screen appears, as shown in Figure 14, the filter's loader MPTfilterLoader.exe is run to complete the steps outlined above. One can then choose a profile and use the application normally. A log file for the filter is located at C:\MPTfilter.log. The filter is unloaded when the application is closed, making the log file accessible to other applications.

Figure 14: Injection of the Filter

When CreateProcessA is called by mPhoneTools.exe, the function CreateProcessADetour of the filter is executed instead. It checks the name of the program being executed. If it is not one of the two subprograms, then the genuine CreateProcessA function call is executed unchanged. Otherwise, the function is executed with the option CREATE_SUSPENDED. This option permits the new process to be created as intended, but places its main thread in the suspended state. This ensures that no data is sent to the phone before the filter is loaded. CreateProcessADetour then injects the filter into the new process using the same technique that the loader of the filter used. Finally, the main thread of the new process is activated using the function ResumeThread.

Note that the filter uses the regular expression engine TRE [12]. The DLL tre.dll must be present on the system for the filter to load and work.

6.3 Filter Operation

mPhoneTools.exe and MMCenter.exe have slightly different architectures. Therefore, the filter works a little differently for each program.

The sequence of operation for mPhoneTools.exe is described in Figure 15. First, the function lineGetIDA is called. The filter's wrapper function lineGetIDADetour is executed instead. It calls the genuine lineGetIDA and stores the returned handle for later use. The communication channel to the phone is now established.

Later on, the program sends a request to the phone using the WriteFile function. If the handle referenced is the handle of the channel previously open, then the data is analyzed by the filter. If the request is deemed safe, the genuine WriteFile is called and the request is sent to the phone. Otherwise, the request is blocked and a forged response is set up for later use as a reply to this request.

Then, the application asks for available data to read on the channel, using the function ClearCommError. The wrapper ClearCommErrorDetour is actually executed instead. It calls the genuine ClearCommError. If data is available on the channel, then the detour function reports it without any change. If not, and if a forged response is waiting for reply, the filter reports that data is available. The amount of data indicated matches the size of the forged response.

The program then calls ReadFileEx, executing the filter's ReadFileExDetour instead. If a forged response is ready for reply and has been reported as available via ClearCommError, and if the size of the data to be read matches the size of the response, then the response is copied to the destination buffer. The completion routine's address is also stored for later use, along with necessary information, such as the thread ID calling ReadFileEx.

Finally, the function SleepEx is called. Its wrapper, SleepExDetour, checks if a callback routine has to be executed and if the calling thread is the same one which called ReadFileEx. If so, the stored completion routine is called to complete the forged response reply.

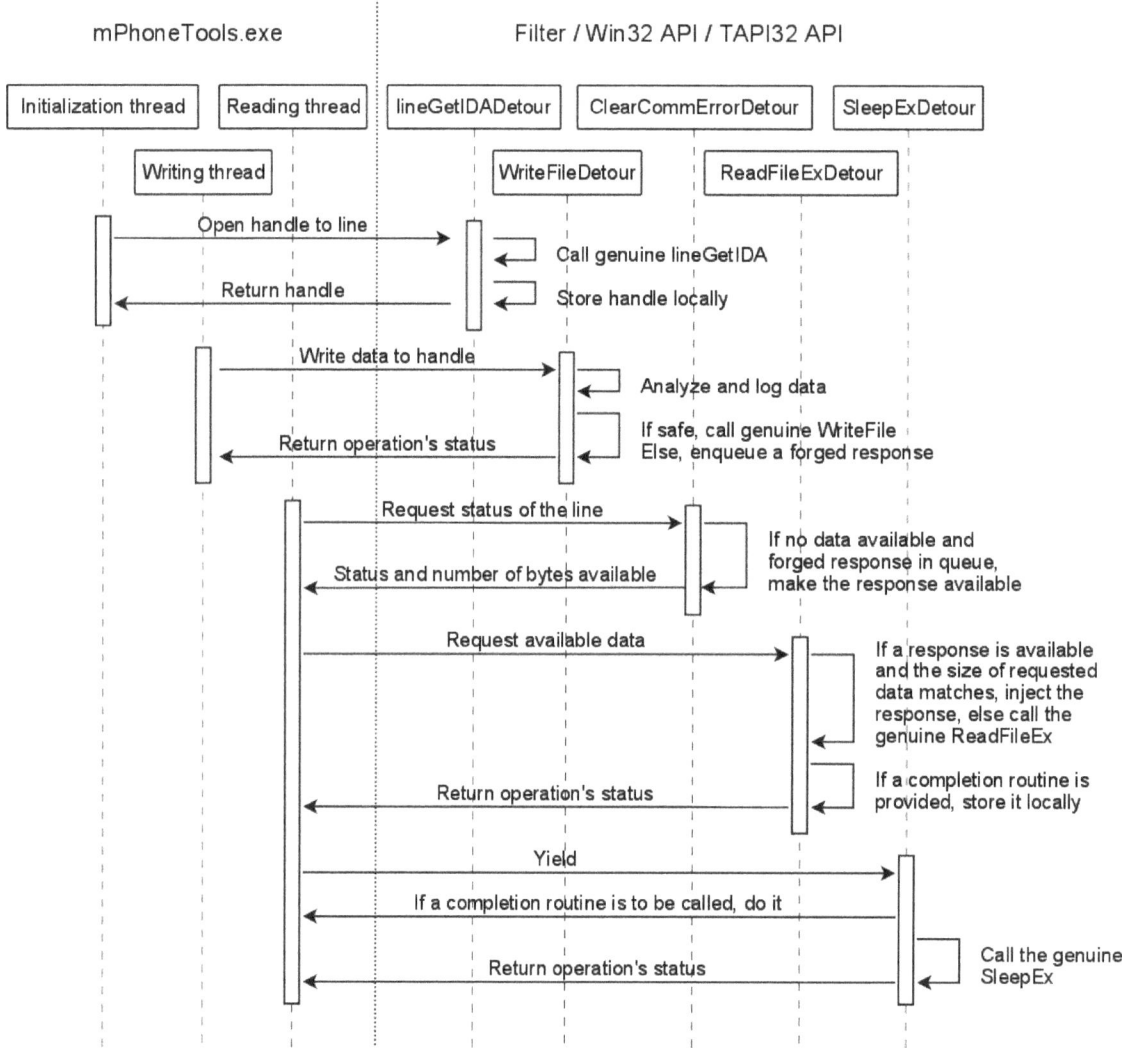

Figure 15: Sequence of Operation for mPhoneTools.exe Filtering

The sequence of operation of MMCenter.exe, illustrated in Figure 16, is similar, except that the function pair WriteFileEx and ReadFile is used instead of WriteFile and ReadFileEx for mPhoneTools.exe. SleepEx is not used at all, since no completion routine can be provided with ReadFile.

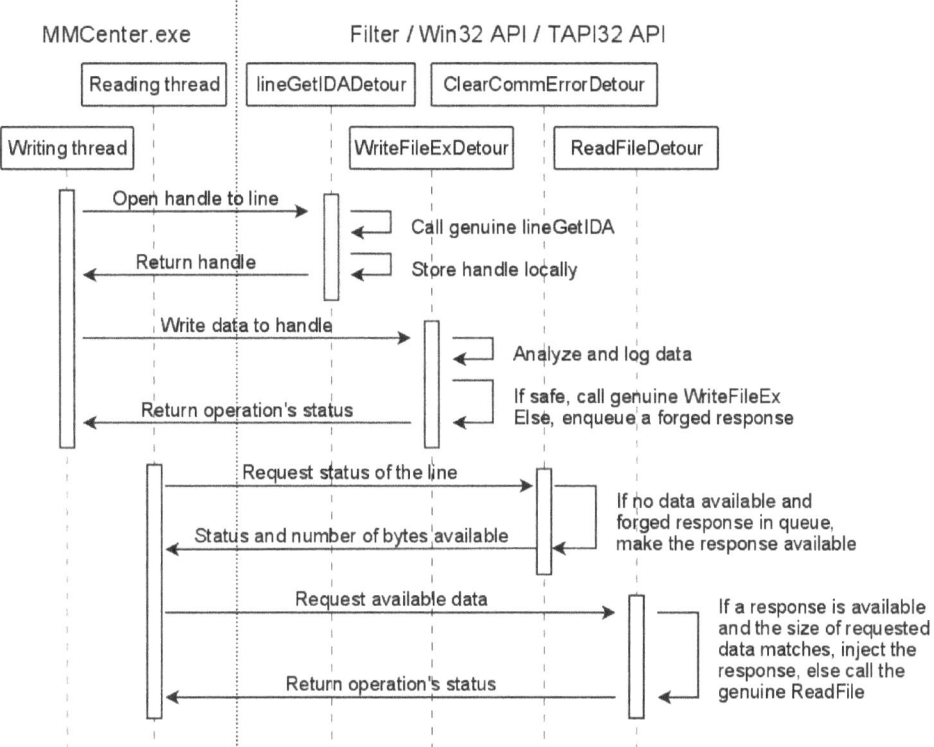

Figure 16: Sequence of Operation for MMCenter.exe Filtering

Most of the traffic sent by MPT involves AT commands, the default protocol used by the application to communicate with the phone. The main work of the filter is done by analyzing the data sent to the device via WriteFile and WriteFileEx. Initially, the filter is in the AT mode. MPT requests to the phone pass through the filter's AT analyzer. The validity of the data unit is checked and the request is compared to the list of allowed AT commands.

Matching the white list of AT commands is implemented through standard regular expressions, using functions from the TRE library. If a match is found, the command is reported as safe and its data unit written to the phone. Otherwise, the command is dropped and a forged response is set up.

When the filter receives an AT command used to switch to OBEX mode, the filter also switches mode to begin processing the OBEX protocol. All OBEX traffic sent by MPT to the phone passes through the filter's OBEX analyzer. Depending on the frame's command code, the request is reported safe or not. The filter allows through only the connect, disconnect, get, set path, and abort operations. In the case of a disconnection, the filter switches back to the AT mode. Responses sent by the phone are not analyzed; they are treated as forensically safe.

7. Conclusions

Cell phone forensics is an emerging discipline. Various impediments exist that create problems for forensic specialists working in this area, and need to be overcome for the discipline to flourish. The technique presented in this paper attempt to resolve the problem with the latency in forensic tool coverage of newly available phone models by phone manager protocol filtering. It is intended as a stopgap measure until forensic tool support for the phone becomes available. For models of phones that due to low popularity or other reasons never gain support from available forensic tools, the technique may also be used as a long-term safeguard for data recovery using a phone manager.

Initial testing of the two prototype implementations indicate that the approach could provide a practical and effective solution for addressing the latency in forensic tool coverage of available phones. The basic technique described is extendable beyond the specific phone manager examples given. Intercepting low-level Windows APIs, as opposed to higher-level internal APIs in the application, allows the solution to be applied to phone managers from other cell phone manufacturers. Reprogramming the filter for the different protocols involved would, of course, be required. As with any forensic tool, the resulting filtered phone manager program requires validation before its use.

8. References

[1] Nokia and Motorola Gain Market Share as Arena Grows, International Herald Tribune, Tech/Media November 22, 2006, <URL: http://www.iht.com/articles/2006/11/22/yourmoney/mobile.php>.

[2] Nokia and Motorola Account for Nearly 50% of Worldwide Sales, Mobiledia, August 25, 2005, <URL: http://www.mobiledia.com/news/35125.html>.

[3] Robert Vamosi, Cell Phone 'CSI,' CNET Reviews, May 25, 2007, <URL: http://reviews.cnet.com/4520-3513_7-6737586-1.htm>.

[4] Annalee Newitz, Courts Cast Wary Eye on Evidence Gleaned From Cell Phones, WIRED, May 10, 2007, <URL: http://www.wired.com/politics/law/news/2007/05/cellphone_forensics>.

[5] Tyler Moore, The Economics of Digital Forensics, Fifth Annual Workshop on the Economics of Information Security, June 2006, <URL: http://www.cl.cam.ac.uk/~twm29/weis06-moore.pdf>.

[6] Galen Hunt, Doug Brubacher, Detours: Binary Interception of Win32 Functions, 3rd USENIX Windows NT Symposium, Seattle, WA, July 1999, <URL: http://research.microsoft.com/~galenh/Publications/HuntUsenixNt99.pdf>.

[7] Wayne Peacock, An Introduction to Nokia F-Bus, Embedtronics, April 2005, <URL: http://www.embedtronics.com/nokia/fbus.html>.

[8] Paul McCarthy, Forensic Analysis of Mobile Phones, BS CIS Thesis, University of South Australia, School of Computer and Information Science, Mawson Lakes, October 2005, <URL: http://esm.cis.unisa.edu.au/new_esml/resources/publications/forensic%20analysis%20of%20mobile%20phones.pdf>.

[9] SincereHacker, DOS Help (Includes obtaining system privileges on windows), July 2007, <URL: http://www.elitehackers.info/forums/showthread.php?p=50838>.

[10] Global cellphone sales slowing, IDC says, CBC News, January 25, 2008, <URL: http://www.cbc.ca/technology/story/2008/01/25/tech-cellphones.html?ref=rss>.

[11] How to create a Windows service by using Sc.exe, Microsoft, Article ID 251192, Revision 3.6, December 5, 2007, <URL: http://support.microsoft.com/kb/251192>.

[12] Ville Laurikari, TRE home page, <URL: http://www.laurikari.net/tre/>.

[13] AT Command set for GSM Mobile Equipment (ME) (Release 1998), 3rd Generation Partnership Project (3GPP) Technical Specification (TS) Group Terminals, 3GPP TS 07.07, version 7.8.0, March 2003, <URL: http://www.3gpp.org/ftp/Specs/archive/07_series/07.07/0707-780.zip>.

Appendix A – Example PCS Filter Log

The example listing is from a simplified log file generated by the PCS filter. Some frames have been removed, as they were not meaningful to demonstrate the performance of the filter, and explanatory text was inserted to highlight interesting protocol exchanges.

The phone used was a Nokia 6101, connected to a computer via a USB Susteen cable. It appears as a serial COM port to the operating system of the computer.

The frames described below are all allowed through the filter, unless explicitly stated. The text in blue describes data sent by the computer to the phone and the text in green the data sent by the phone to the computer. The grey text is for miscellaneous information. Data in orange is especially significant.

In this short example, PCS is used to browse the contact list of the phone, which is empty. Then, the computer is used to add the entry "Voltaire" to the phone's contact list, but the operation is blocked by the filter. Finally, PCS's service is stopped, unloading the filter at the same time.

First, the filter is injected into PCS's service.

```
[03316] DLL loaded
[03316] DLL initialized
```

PCS opens the serial port corresponding to the Susteen cable. The call is intercepted by the filter, which saves the handle of the device for later use.

```
[02376] Serial port open
```

PCS sends a couple of AT commands: one to initialize the phone's modem, and the other to switch into FBUS mode. This information is logged by the detour function filtering the Win32 function "WriteFile".

```
[02724] ATFeedSentFrame: modem initialization
[02724] ATFeedSentFrame: switching to FBUS mode
```

The first FBUS frame is sent to the phone for initialization purposes. From now on, only FBUS frames are used to communicate between the computer and the phone.

```
[02724] FBusFeedSentFrame: FBus session initialization
```

PCS requests the model of the phone, which states it is a Nokia 6101.

```
[02724] FBusFeedSentFrame: phone model requested
[03852] FBusFeedRecvFrame: phone model: "Nokia 6101"
```

Some FBUS frames are exchanged, supposedly to negotiate the upcoming OBEX over FBUS session.

```
[ FBus negotiation related to the OBEX session ]
```

The OBEX over FBUS session is starting. An OBEX CONNECT request is sent to the phone, which replies that the connection has been established.

```
[02492] FBusFeedSentFrame: OBEX request
[02492] ObexFeedSentFrame:        (allowed)
[03852] FBusFeedRecvFrame: OBEX response
[03852] ObexFeedRecvFrame: OBEX connection established
[03852] ObexFeedRecvFrame: request=80 response=a0
[03852] ObexAnalyzePayload: header=cb encoding=4bytes data=2000000
[03852] ObexAnalyzePayload: header=4a encoding=byteseq length=16 data="ùÌ{Ä•<•Ö`NRT"
[03852] f9 ec 7b c4 95 3c 11 d2 98 4e 52 54 00 dc 9e 09
```

PCS asks for the capabilities of the phone using an OBEX request. The phone's OBEX answer consists of XML data. As the amount of information is large, it is split into 17 FBUS frames.

```
[01488] FBusFeedSentFrame: OBEX request
[01488] ObexFeedSentFrame:        (allowed)
[01488] ObexAnalyzePayload: header=cb encoding=4bytes data=2000000
[01488] ObexAnalyzePayload: header=42 encoding=byteseq length=18 data="
                            "
[01488] 78 2d 6f 62 65 78 2f 63 61 70 61 62 69 6c 69 74
[01488] 79 00
[01488] ObexAnalyzePayload: header=4a encoding=byteseq length=8 data="PC Suite"
[01488] 50 43 20 53 75 69 74 65
[03852] FBusFeedRecvFrame: OBEX response { repeated 17 times }
[03852] ObexFeedRecvFrame: request=83 response=a0
[03852] ObexAnalyzePayload: header=c3 encoding=4bytes data=b1070000
[03852] ObexAnalyzePayload: header=49 encoding=byteseq length=1969 data="
<?xml version="1.0" ?>
<!DOCTYPE Capability SYSTEM "obex-capability.dtd">
<Capability Version="1.0">
 <General>
  <Manufacturer>Nokia</Manufacturer>
  <Model>RM-76</Model>
  <SN>356661005704092</SN>
  <SW Version="V 03.35" Date="20050608T120000"/>
  <HW Version="5061"/>
  <Language>en</Language>
  <Memory>
   <MemType>DEV</MemType>
   <!-- DEV memory -->
   <Free>1829696</Free>
   <Used>1539072</Used>
  </Memory>
 </General>
 <Inbox>
  <Object>
   <Type>text/x-vCard</Type>
   <Name-Ext>vcf</Name-Ext>
  </Object>
  <Object>
   <Type>text/x-vCalendar</Type>
   <Name-Ext>vcs</Name-Ext>
  </Object>
 </Inbox>
 <Service>
  <Name>Folder-Browsing</Name>
  <UUID>F9EC7BC4-953c-11d2-984E-525400DC9E09</UUID>
  <Version>1.0</Version>
  <Object>
   <Type>x-obex/folder-listing</Type>
  </Object>
  <Access>
   <Protocol>IrDA</Protocol>
   <Target>F9EC7BC4-953c-11d2-984E-525400DC9E09</Target>
  </Access>
```

```
  <Ext>
   <XNam>Images</XNam>
   <XVal>Folder=C:\Gallery\Images\</XVal>
   <XVal>MemType=DEV</XVal>
  </Ext>
  <Ext>
   <XNam>Videos</XNam>
   <XVal>Folder=C:\Gallery\Video clips\</XVal>
   <XVal>MemType=DEV</XVal>
  </Ext>
  <Ext>
   <XNam>Graphics</XNam>
   <XVal>Folder=C:\Gallery\Graphics\</XVal>
   <XVal>MemType=DEV</XVal>
  </Ext>
  <Ext>
   <XNam>Tones</XNam>
   <XVal>Folder=C:\Gallery\Tones\</XVal>
   <XVal>MemType=DEV</XVal>
  </Ext>
  <Ext>
   <XNam>Recordings</XNam>
   <XVal>Folder=C:\Gallery\Recordings\</XVal>
   <XVal>MemType=DEV</XVal>
  </Ext>
  <Ext>
   <XNam>Applications</XNam>
   <XVal>Folder=C:\predefjava\</XVal>
   <XVal>MemType=DEV</XVal>
  </Ext>
  <Ext>
   <XNam>Games</XNam>
   <XVal>Folder=C:\predefjava\</XVal>
   <XVal>MemType=DEV</XVal>
  </Ext>
 </Service>
 <Service>
  <Name>PCSuite-Settings</Name>
  <Version>1.0</Version>
  <Ext>
   <XNam>SuiteConf</XNam>
   <XVal>File=C:\predefinfofolder\SuiteConf.xml</XVal>
  </Ext>
 </Service>
 <Service>
  <Name>Infolog</Name>
  <Object>
   <Type>x-irmc/info.log</Type>
   <Name-Ext>log</Name-Ext>
  </Object>
 </Service>
 <Service>
  <Name>SyncML</Name>
  <UUID>SYNCML-SYNC</UUID>
  <Version>1.1</Version>
  <Object>
   <Type>application/vnd.syncml+wbxml</Type>
  </Object>
 </Service>
</Capability>"
```

Using OBEX, PCS then requests the listing of the phone's "folder." Similarly, the phone replies by an OBEX answer, consisting of XML data.

```
[03836] FBusFeedSentFrame: OBEX request
[03836] ObexFeedSentFrame:     (allowed)
[03836] ObexAnalyzePayload: header=cb encoding=4bytes data=3000000
```

```
[03836] ObexAnalyzePayload: header=42 encoding=byteseq length=22 data="
        "
[03836] 78 2d 6f 62 65 78 2f 66 6f 6c 64 65 72 2d 6c 69
[03836] 73 74 69 6e 67 00
[03836] ObexAnalyzePayload: header=4a encoding=byteseq length=8 data="PC Suite•AëJ"
[03836] 50 43 20 53 75 69 74 65
[03852] FBusFeedRecvFrame: OBEX response
[03852] ObexFeedRecvFrame: request=83 response=90
[03852] ObexAnalyzePayload: header=c3 encoding=4bytes data=2c010000
[03836] FBusFeedSentFrame: OBEX request
[03836] ObexFeedSentFrame: get (allowed)
[03852] FBusFeedRecvFrame: OBEX response [ repeated 3 times ]
[03852] ObexFeedRecvFrame: request=83 response=a0
[03852] ObexAnalyzePayload: header=49 encoding=byteseq length=300 data="
<?xml version="1.0"?>
<!DOCTYPE folder-listing SYSTEM "obex-folder-listing.dtd"
 [ <!ATTLIST folder mem-type CDATA #IMPLIED>
   <!ATTLIST folder label CDATA #IMPLIED> ]>
<folder-listing version="1.0">
    <folder name="C:" user-perm="R" mem-type="DEV" label="Phone Memory"/>
</folder-listing>"
```

The next set of frames is FBUS. Their purpose is not known precisely, but for this example they are considered to be harmless. They might be used to probe for services on the phone.

```
[02552] FBusFeedSentFrame: unknown request 0
[02552] 1e 00 10 19 00 08 00 03 01 f0 12 00 01 43 1c a1
[03852] FBusFeedRecvFrame: unsupported FBus response (see below)
[03852] 1e 10 00 19 00 0c 03 33 01 f0 13 10 04 55 55 55
[03852] 01 40 5f 96
[02464] FBusFeedSentFrame: unknown request 0
[02464] 1e 00 10 39 00 08 00 03 01 f0 12 00 01 44 1c 86
[03852] FBusFeedRecvFrame: unsupported FBus response (see below)
[03852] 1e 10 00 39 00 0c 03 60 01 f0 13 14 00 00 00 00
[03852] 01 41 0e e0
[04064] FBusFeedSentFrame: unknown request 0
[04064] 1e 00 10 3e 00 08 00 03 01 f0 12 00 01 45 1c 80
[03852] FBusFeedRecvFrame: unsupported FBus response (see below)
[03852] 1e 10 00 3e 00 0c 03 3c 01 f0 13 03 00 00 00 00
[03852] 01 42 0e af
[02552] FBusFeedSentFrame: unknown request 0
[02552] 1e 00 10 22 00 08 00 03 01 f0 12 00 01 46 1c 9f
[03852] FBusFeedRecvFrame: unsupported FBus response (see below)
[03852] 1e 10 00 22 00 0c 03 59 01 f0 13 01 00 55 55 55
[03852] 01 43 5b d5
[02464] FBusFeedSentFrame: unknown request 0
[02464] 1e 00 10 13 00 08 00 03 01 f0 12 00 01 47 1c af
[03852] FBusFeedRecvFrame: unsupported FBus response (see below)
[03852] 1e 10 00 13 00 0c 03 63 01 f0 13 03 09 00 00 00
[03852] 01 44 07 db
[04064] FBusFeedSentFrame: unknown request 0
[04064] 1e 00 10 14 00 08 00 03 01 f0 12 00 01 40 1c af
[03852] FBusFeedRecvFrame: unsupported FBus response (see below)
[03852] 1e 10 00 14 00 0c 03 6b 01 f0 13 00 1e 00 00 00
[03852] 01 45 10 d6
[02552] FBusFeedSentFrame: unknown request 0
[02552] 1e 00 10 02 00 08 00 03 01 f0 12 00 01 41 1c b8
[03852] FBusFeedRecvFrame: unsupported FBus response (see below)
[03852] 1e 10 00 02 00 0c 03 76 01 f0 13 02 0d 55 55 55
[03852] 01 46 56 dc
[02464] FBusFeedSentFrame: unknown request 0
[02464] 1e 00 10 03 00 08 00 03 01 f0 12 00 01 42 1c ba
[03852] FBusFeedRecvFrame: unsupported FBus response (see below)
[03852] 1e 10 00 03 00 0c 03 64 01 f0 13 03 19 00 00 00
[03852] 01 47 17 c9
[04064] FBusFeedSentFrame: unknown request 0
[04064] 1e 00 10 aa 00 08 00 03 01 f0 12 00 01 43 1c 12
[02552] FBusFeedSentFrame: unknown request 0
```

```
[02552] 1e 00 10 01 00 08 00 03 01 f0 12 00 01 44 1c be
[03852] FBusFeedRecvFrame: unsupported FBus response (see below)
[03852] 1e 10 00 01 00 0c 03 73 01 f0 13 04 21 55 55 55
[03852] 01 40 7a da
[02464] FBusFeedSentFrame: unknown request 0
[02464] 1e 00 10 06 00 08 00 03 01 f0 12 00 01 45 1c b8
[03852] FBusFeedRecvFrame: unsupported FBus response (see below)
[03852] 1e 10 00 06 00 0c 03 74 01 f0 13 05 00 00 00 00
[03852] 01 41 0e da
[04064] FBusFeedSentFrame: unknown request 0
[04064] 1e 00 10 1b 00 08 00 03 01 f0 12 00 01 46 1c a6
[03852] FBusFeedRecvFrame: unsupported FBus response (see below)
[03852] 1e 10 00 1b 00 0c 03 39 01 f0 13 04 0d 00 00 00
[03852] 01 42 03 88
```

The next set of frames is also FBUS. It is likely related to browsing the phonebook of the phone, which is treated as harmless in this example.

```
[02552] FBusFeedSentFrame: phone book 1
[03852] FBusFeedRecvFrame: unsupported FBus response (see below)
[03852] 1e 10 00 19 00 60 03 33 01 20 01 0b 05 08 01 00
[03852] 00 01 00 01 05 08 02 00 00 01 00 01 05 08 03 00
[03852] 00 01 00 01 05 08 04 00 00 01 00 01 05 08 05 00
[03852] 00 01 00 02 05 08 06 00 00 0a 00 0a 05 08 07 00
[03852] 00 0a 00 05 05 08 08 00 00 03 00 03 05 08 09 00
[03852] 00 1e 00 1e 05 08 0a 00 00 3f 00 94 05 08 0b 00
[03852] 00 64 00 00 01 43 19 f9
[04064] FBusFeedSentFrame: phone book 1
[03852] FBusFeedRecvFrame: unsupported FBus response (see below)
[03852] 1e 10 00 03 00 7a 03 64 01 26 05 12 1d 00 00 0c
[03852] 07 05 00 64 01 01 00 00 1d 00 00 0c 0b 05 00 64
[03852] 01 05 00 00 1d 00 00 0c 1e 02 00 01 01 01 00 00
[03852] 1d 00 00 0c 09 05 00 fc 00 05 01 00 1d 00 00 0c
[03852] 08 05 00 fc 00 05 01 00 1d 00 00 0c 0a 05 00 fc
[03852] 00 05 01 00 1d 00 00 0c 2c 05 00 fc 00 05 01 00
[03852] 1d 00 00 0c 2e 06 00 0f 00 05 00 00 1d 00 00 0c
[03852] 2f 06 00 02 00 05 00 00 1d 00 00 0c 33 06 02 44
[03852] 1d 70
[03852] FBusFeedRecvFrame: unsupported FBus response (see below)
[03852] 1e 10 00 03 00 68 00 08 00 01 00 00 1d 00 00 0c
[03852] 38 05 00 fc 01 05 01 00 1d 00 00 0c 39 05 00 64
[03852] 01 01 00 00 1d 00 00 0c 3a 06 01 07 00 01 00 00
[03852] 1d 00 00 0c 3d 06 00 01 00 05 00 00 1d 00 00 0c
[03852] 43 03 00 02 00 0a 00 00 1d 00 00 0c 3f 05 00 fc
[03852] 00 05 01 00 1d 00 00 0c 42 00 00 03 00 01 00 00
[03852] 32 00 00 0c 05 02 03 04 06 0a 00 00 01 05 09 16
[02552] FBusFeedSentFrame: phone book 1
[03852] FBusFeedRecvFrame: unsupported FBus response (see below)
[03852] 1e 10 00 03 00 38 03 64 01 26 06 04 1d 00 00 0c
[03852] 07 05 00 20 01 01 00 00 1d 00 00 0c 1e 02 00 01
[03852] 01 01 00 00 1d 00 00 0c 0b 05 00 66 01 01 00 00
[03852] 32 00 00 0c 01 0a 00 00 00 00 00 01 46 26 65
```

PCS is sending an FBUS request to refresh its cache of the phone book.

```
[04064] FBusFeedSentFrame: phone book refresh 1
[03852] FBusFeedRecvFrame: unsupported FBus response (see below)
[03852] 1e 10 00 03 00 10 03 64 01 08 00 01 0f 00 00 08
[03852] 30 00 00 00 01 47 22 21
```

The OBEX session is finally ended using a DISCONNECT request.

```
[03152] FBusFeedSentFrame: OBEX request
```

```
[03152] ObexFeedSentFrame:            (allowed)
[03852] FBusFeedRecvFrame: OBEX response
[03852] ObexFeedRecvFrame: OBEX connection terminated
[03852] ObexFeedRecvFrame: request=81 response=a0
```

More FBUS traffic occurs, supposedly related to the negotiation of the OBEX over FBUS session.

[FBus negociation related to the OBEX session]

Then, another FBUS request, likely related to browsing the phone book is sent and answered. As before, this is treated as a harmless exchange.

```
[04064] FBusFeedSentFrame: phone book 1
[03852] FBusFeedRecvFrame: unsupported FBus response (see below)
[03852] 1e 10 00 19 00 60 03 33 01 20 01 0b 05 08 01 00
[03852] 00 01 00 01 05 08 02 00 00 01 00 01 05 08 03 00
[03852] 00 01 00 01 05 08 04 00 00 01 00 01 05 08 05 00
[03852] 00 01 00 02 05 08 06 00 00 0a 00 0a 05 08 07 00
[03852] 00 0a 00 05 05 08 08 00 00 03 00 03 05 08 09 00
[03852] 00 1e 00 1e 05 08 0a 00 00 3f 00 94 05 08 0b 00
[03852] 00 64 00 00 01 46 19 fc
```

More OBEX over FBUS negotiation occurs.

[FBus negociation related to the OBEX session]

Another OBEX session is established.

```
[00584] FBusFeedSentFrame: OBEX request
[00584] ObexFeedSentFrame:            (allowed)
[03852] FBusFeedRecvFrame: OBEX response
[03852] ObexFeedRecvFrame: request=80 response=5
[03852] FBusFeedRecvFrame: OBEX response
[03852] ObexFeedRecvFrame: OBEX connection established
[03852] ObexFeedRecvFrame: request=80 response=a0
[03852] ObexAnalyzePayload: header=cb encoding=4bytes data=1000000
[03852] ObexAnalyzePayload: header=4a encoding=byteseq length=16 data="0i{Ä•<•Õ˜NKT"
[03852] f9 ec 7b c4 95 3c 11 d2 98 4e 52 54 00 dc 9e 09
```

More FBUS requests are sent to browse the phonebook.

```
[02464] FBusFeedSentFrame: phone book 1
[03852] FBusFeedRecvFrame: unsupported FBus response (see below)
[03852] 1e 10 00 03 00 7a 03 64 01 26 05 12 1d 00 00 0c
[03852] 07 05 00 64 01 01 00 00 1d 00 00 0c 0b 05 00 64
[03852] 01 05 00 00 1d 00 00 0c 1e 02 00 01 01 01 00 00
[03852] 1d 00 00 0c 09 05 00 fc 00 05 01 00 1d 00 00 0c
[03852] 08 05 00 fc 00 05 01 00 1d 00 00 0c 0a 05 00 fc
[03852] 00 05 01 00 1d 00 00 0c 2c 05 00 fc 00 05 01 00
[03852] 1d 00 00 0c 2e 06 00 0f 00 05 00 00 1d 00 00 0c
[03852] 2f 06 00 02 00 05 00 00 1d 00 00 0c 33 06 02 41
[03852] 1d 75
[03852] FBusFeedRecvFrame: unsupported FBus response (see below)
[03852] 1e 10 00 03 00 68 00 08 00 01 00 00 1d 00 00 0c
[03852] 38 05 00 fc 01 05 01 00 1d 00 00 0c 39 05 00 64
[03852] 01 01 00 00 1d 00 00 0c 3a 06 01 07 00 01 00 00
[03852] 1d 00 00 0c 3c 06 00 01 00 05 00 00 1d 00 00 0c
[03852] 43 03 00 02 00 0a 00 00 1d 00 00 0c 3f 05 00 fc
```

```
[03852] 00 05 01 00 1d 00 00 0c 42 06 00 03 00 01 00 00
[03852] 32 00 00 0c 05 02 03 04 06 0a 00 00 01 02 09 11
[02552] FBusFeedSentFrame: phone book 1
[03852] FBusFeedRecvFrame: unsupported FBus response (see below)
[03852] 1e 10 00 03 00 38 03 64 01 26 06 04 1d 00 00 0c
[03852] 07 05 00 20 01 01 00 00 1d 00 00 0c 1e 02 00 01
[03852] 01 01 00 00 1d 00 00 0c 0b 05 00 66 01 01 00 00
[03852] 32 00 00 0c 01 0a 00 00 00 00 00 01 43 26 60
```

At this point, the new contact "Voltaire" is created on the computer, with the associated phone number "12223334444." PCS tries to send an FBUS frame to the filter, which blocks it, since this frame is related to adding a new contact to the phone's contact list and is believed to be potentially harmful. It repeats three times before PCS gives up.

```
[04064] FBusFeedSentFrame: unsupported FBus command (see below)
[04064] 1e 00 10 03 00 0c 00 03 01 15 00 05 00 00 00 00
[04064] 01 42 0e 5e
[04064] FBusFeedSentFrame: unsupported FBus command (see below)
[04064] 1e 00 10 03 00 0c 00 03 01 15 00 05 00 00 00 00
[04064] 01 42 0e 5e
[04064] FBusFeedSentFrame: unsupported FBus command (see below)
[04064] 1e 00 10 03 00 0c 00 03 01 15 00 05 00 00 00 00
[04064] 01 42 0e 5e
```

The new entry is pushed to the phone, using an FBUS request. The strings listed in orange below are the Unicode data encoding for the strings "Voltaire" and "12223334444." This frame is unknown to the filter and therefore blocked. The frame would be definitely harmful if it occurred during a forensics examination. As earlier, PCS tries to send it three times before it gives up.

```
[02464] FBusFeedSentFrame: unsupported FBus command (see below)
[02464] 1e 00 10 03 00 54 00 03 01 0b 00 01 01 00 00 10
[02464] ff 05 ff ff 00 00 00 00 00 00 02 07 00 00 18
[02464] 80 12
[02464]             0b 00 00 24 80 03 00 00 00 18
[02464]
[02464]                   00 00 01 42 03 cf
[02464] FBusFeedSentFrame: unsupported FBus command (see below)
[02464] 1e 00 10 03 00 54 00 03 01 0b 00 01 01 00 00 10
[02464] ff 05 ff ff 00 00 00 00 00 00 02 07 00 00 18
[02464] 80 12 00 56 00 6f 00 6c 00 74 00 61 00 69 00 72
[02464] 00 65 00 00 0b 00 00 24 80 03 00 00 00 18 00 31
[02464] 00 32 00 32 00 32 00 33 00 33 00 33 00 34 00 34
[02464] 00 34 00 34 00 00 00 00 01 42 03 cf
[02464] FBusFeedSentFrame: unsupported FBus command (see below)
[02464] 1e 00 10 03 00 54 00 03 01 0b 00 01 01 00 00 10
[02464] ff 05 ff ff 00 00 00 00 00 00 02 07 00 00 18
[02464] 80 12 00 56 00 6f 00 6c 00 74 00 61 00 69 00 72
[02464] 00 65 00 00 0b 00 00 24 80 03 00 00 00 18 00 31
[02464] 00 32 00 32 00 32 00 33 00 33 00 33 00 34 00 34
[02464] 00 34 00 34 00 00 00 00 01 42 03 cf
```

This is the same frame sent earlier when the contact "Voltaire" was created and blocked each time, as before.

```
[02552] FBusFeedSentFrame: unsupported FBus command (see below)
[02552] 1e 00 10 03 00 0c 00 03 01 17 00 05 00 00 00 00
[02552] 01 42 0e 5c
[02552] FBusFeedSentFrame: unsupported FBus command (see below)
[02552] 1e 00 10 03 00 0c 00 03 01 17 00 05 00 00 00 00
[02552] 01 42 0e 5c
[02552] FBusFeedSentFrame: unsupported FBus command (see below)
```

```
[02552] 1e 00 10 03 00 0c 00 03 01 17 00 05 00 00 00 00
[02552] 01 42 0e 5c
```

The second OBEX session is ended.

```
[00560] FBusFeedSentFrame: OBEX request
[00560] ObexFeedSentFrame:            (allowed)
[03852] FBusFeedRecvFrame: OBEX response
[03852] ObexFeedRecvFrame: OBEX connection terminated
[03852] ObexFeedRecvFrame: request=81 response=a0
```

More FBUS negotiation for the OBEX session occurs.

```
[ FBus negotiation related to the OBEX session ]
```

PCS sends an FBUS frame to have the phone's modem switch back to AT mode.

```
[02768] FBusFeedSentFrame: switching back to AT mode
```

PCS's service is stopped. Hence the filter is unloaded at the same time.

```
[03280] DLL unloaded
```

Appendix B – Example MPT Filter Log

The example listing is from a simplified log file generated by the MPT filter. Some frames have been removed, as they were not meaningful to demonstrate the performance of the filter, and explanatory text was inserted to highlight interesting protocol exchanges.

The phone used was a Motorola v180, connected to a computer via a USB Susteen cable. The phone appears like a modem in the Windows device list.

The frames described below are all allowed through the filter, unless explicitly stated. The text in blue describes data sent by the computer to the phone and the text in green the data sent by the phone to the computer. The grey text is for miscellaneous information. Data in orange is especially significant.

In this short example, MPT is used to browse the contact list of the phone, then to add the entry "Rousseau."

First, the filter is injected into mPhoneTools.exe.

```
[00304] DllMain: DLL loaded
[00304] ATInit: initializing the regex...
[00304] ATInit: done
[00304] DllMain: DLL initialized
```

The line to the phone is opened by calling lineGetIDA.

```
[03372] lineGetIDADetour: line to the phone opened
```

A large sequence of commands is sent to gather information from the phone.

```
[03164] ATFilter: request allowed through "AT&F"
[03164] ATFilter: request allowed through "AT+MODE=0"
[03164] ATFilter: request allowed through "ATE0Q0V1"
[03164] ATFilter: request allowed through "ATS0=0"
[03164] ATFilter: request allowed through "ATX4&C1"
[03164] ATFilter: request allowed through "ATE0+FCLASS=0"
[03164] ATFilter: request allowed through "AT+CBST=7,0,0"
[03164] ATFilter: request allowed through "AT+CBST=7,0,1"
[03164] ATFilter: request allowed through "AT+CRC=0"
[03164] ATFilter: request allowed through "ATE0"
[03164] ATFilter: request allowed through "ATE0"
[03164] ATFilter: request allowed through "AT+CSCS=""ASCII"""
[03164] ATFilter: request allowed through "AT+CPBS=""ME"""
[03164] ATFilter: request allowed through "AT+CPBR=?"
[03164] ATFilter: request allowed through "AT+CPBS=""SM"""
[03164] ATFilter: request allowed through "AT+CPBR=?"
[03164] ATFilter: request allowed through "AT+CGMI;+CGMM;+CGMR;+CGSN"
[03164] ATFilter: request allowed through "AT+CIMI"
[03164] ATFilter: request allowed through "AT+CNUM?"
[03164] ATFilter: request allowed through "AT+CPMS=""MT"""
[03164] ATFilter: request allowed through "AT+CPMS=""IM"""
[03164] ATFilter: request allowed through "AT+CBST=?"
[03164] ATFilter: request allowed through "AT+CSCA?"
[03164] ATFilter: request allowed through "ATE0"
[03164] ATFilter: request allowed through "AT+MODE=0"
[03164] ATFilter: request allowed through "AT+MDBL=0"
[03164] ATFilter: request allowed through "AT+CGMI;+CGMM;+CGMR;+CGSN"
[03164] ATFilter: request allowed through "AT+CSQ;+CBC"
```

```
[03164] ATFilter: request allowed through "ATE0"
[03164] ATFilter: request allowed through "AT+MODE=0"
[03164] ATFilter: request allowed through "AT+MDBL=0"
[03164] ATFilter: request allowed through "AT+CGMI;+CGMM;+CGMR;+CGSN"
[03164] ATFilter: request allowed through "AT+CSQ;+CBC"
[03164] ATFilter: request allowed through "AT+CPMS=""IM"""
[03164] ATFilter: request allowed through "AT+CPBS=""ME"""
[03164] ATFilter: request allowed through "AT+CPBR=?"
[03164] ATFilter: request allowed through "AT+CPBS?"
[03164] ATFilter: request allowed through "AT+CPBS=""SM"""
[03164] ATFilter: request allowed through "AT+CPBR=?"
[03164] ATFilter: request allowed through "AT+CPBS?"
[03164] ATFilter: request allowed through "AT+CPBS=""ME"""
[03164] ATFilter: request allowed through "AT+CPBS?"
```

Execution of the subprogram MOffice.exe occurs. The filter injects itself in the new process.

```
[03616] CreateProcessADetour: new process creation request
[03616] "C:\Program Files\Motorola Phone Tools\MOffice.EXE"  /P=263532 /I=9[03616]
[03616] CreateProcessADetour: injecting the DLL in the new process...
[03616] E:\My Documents\Visual Studio
2005\Projects\MPTfilter\release\MPTfilterLibrary.dll[03616]
[03616] CreateProcessADetour: the DLL injection succeeded
```

The filter in the new process is initialized.

```
[02732] DllMain: DLL loaded
[02732] ATInit: initializing the regex...
[02732] ATInit: done
[02732] DllMain: DLL initialized
```

Another large number of AT commands are sent to the phone. Some of them are used to gather the contact list.

```
[...]
[03164] ATFilter: request allowed through "AT+MPBR=1,100"
[03164] ATFilter: request allowed through "AT+MPBR=101,200"
[03164] ATFilter: request allowed through "AT+MPBR=201,300"
[03164] ATFilter: request allowed through "AT+MPBR=301,400"
[03164] ATFilter: request allowed through "AT+MPBR=401,500"
[03164] ATFilter: request allowed through "AT+MODE=0"
[03164] ATFilter: request allowed through "AT+MODE=2"
[03164] ATFilter: request allowed through "ATE0"
[03164] ATFilter: request allowed through "AT+CSCS=""UCS2"""
[03164] ATFilter: request allowed through "AT+CSCS?"
[03164] ATFilter: request allowed through "AT+CPBS=""SM"""
[03164] ATFilter: request allowed through "AT+CPBR=501,600"
[03164] ATFilter: request allowed through "AT+CPBR=601,700"
[03164] ATFilter: request allowed through "AT+CPBR=701,754"
[...]
```

The entry "Rousseau" is pushed to the phone's contact list and blocked by the filter.

```
[03164] ATFilter: REQUEST BLOCKED
"AT+MPBW=3,"10002223333",129,"          ",0,0,255,0,0,1"
```

A forged response is built and injected, so the calling program thinks the operation succeeded.

```
[04016] ReadFileExDetour: injecting a forged response
```

Another large set of commands is sent and then the application is closed.

```
[03164] ATFilter: request allowed through "AT+MODE=0"
[03164] ATFilter: request allowed through "AT+MODE=2"
[…]
[03164] DllMain: DLL unloaded
```

In this next example, MMCenter.exe is executed to demonstrate the filtering of OBEX traffic.

First, the process MMCenter.exe is created and the filter is injected and initialized.

```
[…]
[04036] CreateProcessADetour: new process creation request
[04036] "C:\Program Files\Motorola Phone Tools\MMCenter.EXE"  /P=1967468[04036]
[04036] CreateProcessADetour: injecting the DLL in the new process...
[04036] E:\My Documents\Visual Studio
2005\Projects\MPTfilter\release\MPTfilterLibrary.dll[04036]
[04036] CreateProcessADetour: the DLL injection succeeded
[01648] DllMain: DLL loaded
[01648] ATInit: initializing the regex...
[01648] ATInit: done
[01648] DllMain: DLL initialized
```

The new process opens a line to the phone.

```
[03368] lineGetIDADetour: line to the phone opened
```

The application sends the AT command AT+MODE=22 to instruct the phone to switch to OBEX.

```
[03368] ATFilter: switching to OBEX
```

The OBEX connection is established with an OBEX CONNECT frame.

```
[03368] OBEXFilter: frame allowed through
[03368] 80 00 1a 12 00 04 00 46 00 13 f9 ec 7b c4 95 3c
[03368] 11 d2 98 4e 52 54 00 dc 9e 09
```

OBEX commands are sent to browse the phone's repository.

```
[03368] OBEXFilter: frame allowed through
[03368] 85 00 0d 02 00 cb 00 00 00 00 01 00 03
[03368] OBEXFilter: frame allowed through
[03368] 83 00 26 cb 00 00 00 00 01 00 05 00 00 42 00 19
[03368] 78 2d 6f 62 65 78 2f 66 6f 6c 64 65 72 2d 6c 69
[03368] 73 74 69 6e 67 00
[00772] OBEXFilter: frame allowed through
[00772] 83 00 03
[00772] OBEXFilter: frame allowed through
[00772] 83 00 03
[03368] OBEXFilter: frame allowed through
```

```
[03368] 85 00 1d 02 00 cb 00 00 00 00 01 00 13 00 70 00
[03368] 69 00 63 00 74 00 75 00 72 00 65 00 00
[03368] OBEXFilter: frame allowed through
[03368] 83 00 26 cb 00 00 00 00 01 00 05 00 00 42 00 19
[03368] 78 2d 6f 62 65 78 2f 66 6f 6c 64 65 72 2d 6c 69
[03368] 73 74 69 6e 67 00
[00772] OBEXFilter: frame allowed through
[00772] 83 00 03
[00772] OBEXFilter: frame allowed through
[00772] 83 00 03
[03368] OBEXFilter: frame allowed through
[03368] 85 00 0a 03 00 cb 00 00 00 00
[03368] OBEXFilter: frame allowed through
[03368] 83 00 26 cb 00 00 00 00 01 00 05 00 00 42 00 19
[03368] 78 2d 6f 62 65 78 2f 66 6f 6c 64 65 72 2d 6c 69
[03368] 73 74 69 6e 67 00
[00772] OBEXFilter: frame allowed through
[00772] 83 00 03
[00772] OBEXFilter: frame allowed through
[00772] 83 00 03
[03368] OBEXFilter: frame allowed through
[03368] 85 00 1d 02 00 cb 00 00 00 00 01 00 13 00 70 00
[03368] 69 00 63 00 74 00 75 00 72 00 65 00 00
[03368] OBEXFilter: frame allowed through
[03368] 83 00 26 cb 00 00 00 00 01 00 05 00 00 42 00 19
[03368] 78 2d 6f 62 65 78 2f 66 6f 6c 64 65 72 2d 6c 69
[03368] 73 74 69 6e 67 00
[00772] OBEXFilter: frame allowed through
[00772] 83 00 03
[00772] OBEXFilter: frame allowed through
[00772] 83 00 03
```

A request for a file deletion is blocked by the filter. The opcode 0x82 is for OBEX PUT.

```
[03368] OBEXFilter: FRAME BLOCKED
[03368]    00 25 cb 00 00 00 00 01 00 1d 00 49 00 6d 00
[03368] 61 00 67 00 65 00 30 00 30 00 30 00 2e 00 6a 00
[03368] 70 00 67 00 00
```

A forged response is injected, to let the program think that the operation succeeded.

```
[00772] ReadFileDetour: injecting a forged response
```

Other browsing operations are performed.

```
[...]
[03368] OBEXFilter: frame allowed through
[03368] 83 00 26 cb 00 00 00 00 01 00 05 00 00 42 00 19
[03368] 78 2d 6f 62 65 78 2f 66 6f 6c 64 65 72 2d 6c 69
[03368] 73 74 69 6e 67 00
[00772] OBEXFilter: frame allowed through
[00772] 83 00 03
[00772] OBEXFilter: frame allowed through
[00772] 83 00 03
```

The application ends the session, sending an OBEX DISCONNECT request to the phone, which switches it back to AT mode.

```
[02752] OBEXFilter: switching back to AT
[02752] OBEXFilter: frame allowed through
[02752] 81 00 08 cb 00 00 00 00
```

The application is closed.

```
[03368] DllMain: DLL unloaded
```

www.ingramcontent.com/pod-product-compliance
Lightning Source LLC
Chambersburg PA
CBHW081801170526
45167CB00008B/3283